FISHERMEN

CAREERS

William Russell

The Rourke Press, Inc.
Vero Beach, Florida 32964

Edited by Sandra A. Robinson

PHOTO CREDITS
All photos © Lynn M. Stone

Library of Congress Cataloging-in-Publication Data

Russell, William, 1942-
    Fishermen / by William Russell.
    p. cm. — (Careers)
    Includes index.
    ISBN 1-57103-055-7
    1. Fisheries—Vocational guidance—Juvenile literature.
[1. Fisheries—Vocational guidance. 2. Vocational guidance.
 3. Fishing.] I. Title. II. Series: Russell, William, 1942-   Careers.
SH331.9.R87 1994
639.2'023—dc20   93-42483
                                                           CIP
Printed in the USA   AC

0.001

TABLE OF CONTENTS

Fishermen	5
What Fishermen Do	6
Who Can Be a Fisherman?	9
Where Fishermen Work	11
Guiding	14
The Guide's Gear	16
Commercial Fishermen	19
Shellfish Fishermen	20
Learning to Be a Fisherman	22
Glossary	23
Index	24

FISHERMEN

Pelicans aren't the only ones who go fishing nearly every day. Fishing is a full-time job for many people.

Professional, or paid, fishermen enjoy the outdoors, and being on and around water. However, fishing for a living is not very much like fishing for fun on a family vacation. In fact, many people who work as fishermen never handle a fishing pole!

When it's an everyday job, fishing can be cold, hard, slippery work.

With the same taste for fish as the human fishermen on deck, a pelican hitches a ride on a Florida charter boat

WHAT FISHERMEN DO

People who fish for fun are sport fishermen. **Commercial** fishermen are paid to catch large numbers of fish to sell to stores and restaurants.

Fishing is a job to wilderness guides and **charter** boat captains, too. Wilderness fishing guides take small numbers of sport fishermen into rugged, **remote** areas. Charter boat captains hire, or charter, their boats to groups of sport fishermen.

Commercial fishermen in Massachusetts pull cod from a fish box

WHO CAN BE A FISHERMAN?

A commercial fisherman has to spend long days — or weeks — at sea. The person also has to do hard work in cold, wet conditions.

A wilderness guide must know as much about back country streams and lakes, as the bears who live there do. The guide must also be an expert sport fisherman.

A charter captain must own a good-sized boat or work for someone who does. He or she must be an expert sailor.

Braving a snowstorm, commercial fishermen head to sea in Alaska

WHERE FISHERMEN WORK

Most commercial fishermen work on large boats that sail the ocean. A few commercial boats fish large rivers and lakes.

Commercial fishermen live in **port,** or coastal, cities. Their boats sail from these ports to good fishing areas and then return to sell their catch.

Wilderness fishing guides travel into out-of-the-way places where people are scarce.

Charter boat captains make day-long trips from coastal cities.

Commercial fishing boats in the port town of Seldovia, Alaska

*A wilderness fishing guide shows cooking know-how
with salmon and lake trout on an open fire*

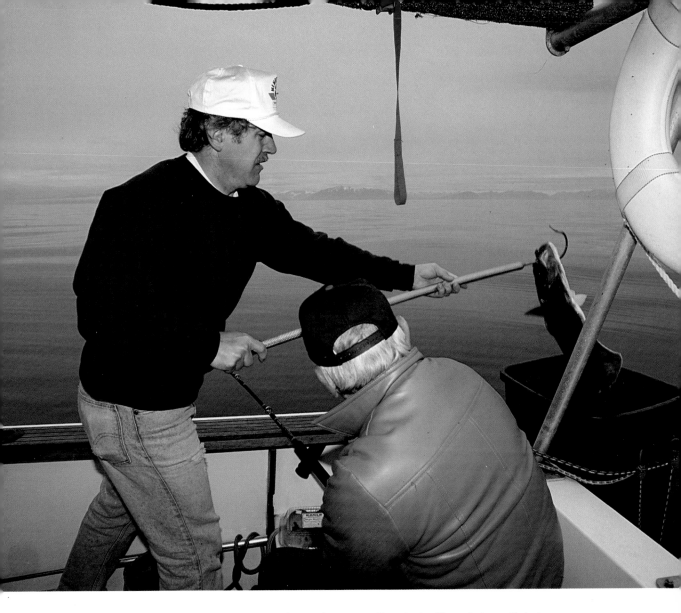

The charter boat captain swings a client's halibut into a fish box

GUIDING

Clients, the people who pay a wilderness fishing guide, hire their guide for many reasons. The most important is that the guide knows the area and the clients don't. The guide also knows how the area should be fished.

A good wilderness guide can lead clients to great fishing. He or she can also clean the fish that are caught, prepare meals, and provide camping equipment.

After netting it, a guide hands his client a silver prize

THE GUIDE'S GEAR

Guides and charter boat captains are usually too busy to fish themselves. They spend their time working with clients and with their gear, or equipment. The guide or captain has to manage a boat and motor, fishing tackle, food, safety equipment and other things.

Guides and charter boat captains who fish the sea, for example, have to understand **navigational** systems. Modern navigational instruments will show the boat captain a safe route home, even in fog or darkness.

A charter boat captain studies his course in Alaska seas

COMMERCIAL FISHERMEN

Most commercial fishermen sail on large boats run by several fishermen. A few commercial fishermen work by themselves from small boats.

Commercial fishermen generally catch fish in huge nets. Fishermen catch some tuna and other kinds of fish on long lines with dozens of baited hooks.

On large boats, called "floating fish factories," fishermen clean and freeze their fish at sea.

Commercial fishermen in Maine straighten their nets for another day of fishing

SHELLFISH FISHERMEN

Some commercial "fishermen" catch **shellfish.**
Certain hard-shelled sea animals, such as crabs
and lobsters, are called shell*fish* — but they are not
really fish.

Shellfish fishermen bait wooden and steel traps
with meat and lower them onto the sea bottom.
Lobsters and crabs can crawl into the traps but
cannot escape.

*A Maine lobster fisherman
paddles to his lobster boat*

LEARNING TO BE A FISHERMAN

Commercial fishermen learn their jobs from other fishermen. Commercial fishermen often have relatives who have worked at sea.

A person who loves to fish in a wilderness area may decide to share the interest with others. He or she may become a guide.

Charter boat captains have a keen love and knowledge of the sea or a large lake. They must pass a Coast Guard test on boating skills before starting a charter business.

Glossary

charter (CHAR ter) — a boat for hire; to hire a boat

client (KLI ent) — a person who hires the services of another

commercial (kuh MUR shul) — referring to work that is done to earn money

navigational (nahv uh GAY shun ul) — referring to instruments used to find locations and routes

port (PORT) — a city or place of shelter along a coast

professional (pro FESH un ul) — a person who is trained and paid for doing a job

remote (re MOTE) — somewhere far away or out-of-the-way

shellfish (SHELL fish) — various hard-shelled sea animals, including crabs, lobsters, oysters, clams and shrimp

INDEX

boats   6, 9, 11, 16, 19
charter boat captains   6, 9, 11,
    16, 22
clients   14, 16
crabs   20
fish   6, 11, 14, 19, 20
fishermen
    commercial   6, 9, 11, 19, 20, 22
    sport   6, 9
fishing   5, 14
guides   6, 9, 11, 14, 16, 22
lakes   9, 11, 22
lobsters   20
navigational systems   16
nets   19

ocean   9, 11, 16, 19, 22
ports   11
rivers   11
sea (see *ocean*)
shellfish   20
traps   20
tuna   19